INTRODUCTION TO ALGO TRADING – HOW RETAIL TRADERS CAN SUCCESSFULLY COMPETE WITH PROFESSIONAL TRADERS

By Kevin J. Davey

ISBN 9781981038350 (Paperback)

Kevin J. Davey
Visit my website at www.AOKbooks.com

Printed in the United States of America

First Printing: May 2018

DISCLAIMER

By Kevin J. Davey

CONTENTS

NOTE: To see figures full size, and in color, you can download them right here:
http://www.aokbooks.com/introalgobookfigs.zip

INTRODUCTION

6:20 AM Saturday morning could not come quickly enough. That was usually the time I would hear the familiar "thunk" of a rolled up copy of the Los Angeles Times newspaper hitting my condo's front door. That was if the delivery person had good aim that day. Some days the bushes nearby would welcome the paper with open arms (branches?) instead. Other days the newspaper never arrived at all. But on this Saturday I heard the paper hit the door, and when I did, I knew it was time to prepare for Monday's trading.

Scrambling out of bed, I opened the door, grabbed the newspaper, and tore it apart until I found the Business section. Towards the back was the data I was looking for – the information that would, in a short time, make me fabulously wealthy (or so I thought): the daily commodity prices for the previous day.

As you may have guessed, this was back before computers took over and daily and intraday data was accessible with a few keystrokes. This was old school to the max – everything was on paper!

Anyhow, I scanned the commodity prices and found the prices for Live Hogs, as it was called back then (it is Lean Hogs now). I took the closing price for the nearest month's contract, and copied it to a paper sheet that had 6 columns in it: date, closing price, 4 period average, 9 period average, 14 period average and signal.

I diligently calculated each average by hand – remember, I had no computer to help me back then – and then I compared the results to my rules:

9 period average greater than the 14 period average? Yes!

4 period average greater than the 9 period average? Yes!!

Closing price crossing above the 4 period average? Yes!!!!

That was it – everything was yes and I had a long signal! Monday morning, I would place an order to buy 1 live hog contract at the market. I dutifully wrote "GO LONG" in the signal column, cementing the trade in my mind.

JUNE 92 LIVE HOGS

DATE	CLOSE	4 AVG.	9 AVG	14 AVG.	SIGNAL?
3/2/1992	44.52				
3/3	44.35				
3/4	45.1				
3/5	45.7				
3/6	46.57	45.285			
3/9 Mon	46.52	45.827			
3/10	46.25	46.12			
3/11	46.1	46.352			
3/12	46.35	46.21			
3/13	46.17	46.222	45.835		
3/16 Mon	46.25	46.217	46.05		
3/17	46.1	46.217	46.161		
3/18	46.3	46.205	46.283		
3/19	46.25	46.225	46.257	45.855	
3/20	46.35	46.25	46.288	45.986	GO LONG!!

Figure 1- Old School Algo Trading, By Hand!

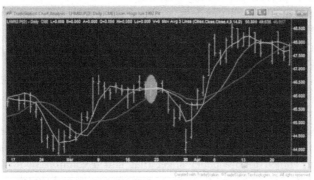

Figure 2- Algo Buy Signal, With Modern Technology

I was nervous, excited and in a dream state the rest of the weekend – my first real commodity trade!

I did not know it, but even back in those old days I was trading algorithmically, or "algo" trading. I was trading according to a precise set a rules, which when you boil it down, is all algorithmic trading really is.

Back then, traders referred to it as systematic trading, mechanical trading or rules based trading. A few years ago, many people spoke of robot or "bot" trading.

But until recently, very few used the term algorithmic. Yet, it is all basically the same thing.

So, realize whenever someone mentions one of these terms – mechanical, systematic, rule based or algorithmic trading - they are likely referring to the same thing: a set of rules that tell you when to enter and exit a trade. These rules could be on a computer, in your head, or as was the case for me in the early days, written on good ol' paper.

That is the first lesson of this book – **algo trading = rules to trade by**.

There are many more lessons in this book, all designed to introduce you to the world of algorithmic trading. This type of trading applies for many different instruments: stocks, ETFs, forex, futures, and options to name a few. Don't let the terms algorithmic or algo scare you; in this book I'll walk you through the basics of algorithmic trading:

- A Discussion of What Exactly Algo Trading Is, and What It Is Not
- The Basics of Algo Trading, For Beginner to Intermediate Traders
- Figuring Out If Algo Trading Is Something You Should Consider
- The Many Advantages of Algo Trading
- The Disadvantages of Algo Trading
- How To Begin Algo Trading On Your Own
- Selecting a Trading Software Platform
- Learning the Basics Of Your Platform
- Learning To Program In Your Platform's Language
- A Simple Algo To Get You Started
- Tips For Successful Algorithmic Trading
- Steps To Take After You Read This Book

The intent of this book is not to teach you the basics of trading in general; there are plenty of other books available on that subject. This book is intended to get you started with algo trading, with the assumption you know some trading basics. I feel strongly that algo trading is a great way for smaller retail traders to compete against professional traders.

By the end of the book, you won't be scared off when people talk about trading algos. You'll know the basics, and also have a plan for your future endeavors in algorithmic trading.

With that, let's get started on the journey!

CHAPTER 1 – THE DIFFERENT TYPES OF TRADING

"Algos" and "algorithms." These two words strike fear into the hearts of many a trader. Visions of computer programs running wild, buying and selling with reckless abandon, are a common nightmare. A trader goes to sleep flat, and wakes up to find a rogue robot algorithm frittered away his or her account, buying and selling all night, due to a simple programming bug.

Figure 3– A Trading Robot Run Amuck?

Or worse yet, the trader wakes up to find he is short 100 ES (mini S&P) contracts, when he only wanted to be short one contract!

Maybe instead your nightmare vision is of hedge funds, executing "killer bot" algos with lightning speed, draining the accounts of all the slower traders.

The truth, of course, is that trading algos can do those things, and worse. Horror stories abound of these sorts of account killing computer codes. These exact nightmare scenarios have happened. But, properly designed algos can also be friendly, too.

I obviously will focus on the friendly algos!

But before I dive into details of algos, it is important to discuss some of the different types of trading. That will help you understand what an algo is, what it can do, and most importantly, what it cannot do.

Discretionary Trading

Most retail people out there are discretionary traders. Discretionary simply means traders use some sort of judgment to enter and exit trades.

For example, a trader hears about a hot stock on CNBC, and immediately decides to buy some. That is discretionary trading.

Another trader has a chart that she stares at all day. It may be filled with indicators, trendlines, moving averages, etc. Or it may be naked, except for price data. Once that trader makes a trade decision based on all she sees, that is a discretionary trade.

Our third trader has a DOM ladder only, a visual tool which shows all the resting buy and sell orders along with prices. He trades based on this tool. He is likely a discretionary trader, too.

At the end of the day, if you asked any of these traders about why they took certain trades, and why they avoided taking other trades (that may have looked exactly the same), they might give you a "deer in the headlights" look, or a vague response like "I don't know, it just felt right!"

The truth is discretionary traders may or may not have rules, they may or may not follow these rules, and they may not be consistent in applying these rules. Heck, they might not even be able to describe the rules that caused them to trade.

I remember being in a trading room with a "price action" guru a while back. He was calling the market live, and it went something like this: "yes, the market is looking weak, and there is a short setup here that I usually take, so I am just waiting for a short entry...waiting...waiting...no, it's a long trade! I just got out with a profit!"

Huh?

When asked about it later, the guru could not explain how a textbook (according to him) short entry suddenly turned into a profitable long scalp trade. "It just felt right," he explained.

It made me wonder if he was even live trading, but that is another story. The point is that he was trading (likely simulated trading) in a discretionary fashion.

Discretionary trading, then, involves trading decisions that involve some degree of human judgment. Maybe it is intuition, or a sixth sense, or even random guessing, but the trade selection usually includes something that can't quite be defined or tested.

Now, that type of trading might sound wrong to you ("who trades based on intuition?") or it may sound appealing ("great, I get to use my brain to help me decide!"). But the fact is many people do it, and some people are successful at it. It is a legitimate way to trade.

Yet discretionary trading is definitely NOT algorithmic trading.

I'm guessing, if you are reading this book, chances are you might have already tried and failed at discretionary trading. Don't feel bad, I count myself in your ranks – I was never a good discretionary trader. That is the main reason I dove into algo trading.

Algorithmic Trading

Algo trading is all about rules. In fact, it is nothing but rules. No discretion. No human judgment.

Trading algorithms can be as simple as you want, or as complicated as you want.

How simple? Here is a basic 2 line strategy:

If close < average close of last 5 bars, go long
If close > average close of last 5 bars, go short

Figure 4 - Buy/Sell Signals For A Simple Algo

Over the past 13 years, this strategy would have made over $92,000 after slippage and commissions, trading just one contract! And it makes money on both the long and short side! Don't get too excited though, the last few years have not been kind to this strategy...

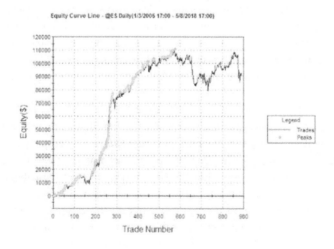

Figure 5 - A Simple (But Not Consistently Profitable) Algo Equity Curve

By Kevin J. Davey

Figure 6 - Typical Algo Performance Report

That was a very simple algo. In contrast, algorithmic strategies can also be extremely complicated, too. There are traders with single algorithms that run 25,000 lines of code or more – real rocket science stuff!

There are two keys to trading algorithms:

1. They can be tested. Most algorithms can be historically tested, commonly referred to as a backtest. This turns out to be a major advantage of creating algorithms, which I'll describe later. For algos that cannot be historically tested, they almost always can be live tested in simulation mode, with proper precautions and some caveats. In either case, the trader can usually determine the acceptability of the strategy BEFORE trading it with real money.

2. Algorithms are rigidly defined. If the algorithm sees a long setup today, it will tell you to go long. If it sees that same setup tomorrow, it will tell you to go long again. The algo only looks at what it was programmed to look at. It doesn't care what the Fed thinks, does not care about the news, and does not care that Jim Cramer screamed that a certain stock was a buy last night – unless, of course, you program those types of rules into your algorithm. The algo is consistent in how it follows the rules.

Many traders speak of "black boxes," a special type of algorithm. With black boxes, the rules (the algorithm) remain hidden to the trader. He or she only gets the entry and exit signals, and has no idea how those signals were produced.

That type of algorithm might sound unappealing or scary, but many people like that approach. It is really hard to interfere with computer code you cannot even see!

Some Examples Of Algo Trading

So what does an algo trader look like? Here are some typical examples:

- A retail trader, trading at home. He works full time, so trading is his hobby. Every night, he downloads the latest prices, calculates his signals either by hand or on a computer, and places trades according to the rules. He may or may not check positions during the day, but since he places orders during non-work hours, he knows he is following his strategies each and every day.

- A prop trader, trading full time. He enters and exits trades all day long, again according to set rules. He never, ever deviates from the rules, since he knows his boss spot checks his trades for adherence to the rules.

- A hedge fund computer code, written by numerous PhDs in math, statistics and physics. The computer code they run has 50,000 lines of code, and does everything – enter trades, exits trades, calculates position sizing, automatically performs rollovers, etc. A junior trader is always nearby, monitoring trades in case of a malfunction, but the computer controls the show. The strategies they run can be on the order of microseconds (in and out quickly), to day trades of a few hours, to swing trades lasting weeks.

- A professional retail trader, using a standard retail platform, Tradestation. He creates strategies, then lets Tradestation run those strategies automated. He is usually closely monitoring positions, because as Tradestation personnel say "automated trading does not mean unattended trading." He can trade quite a few automated strategies, assuming he has enough capital, and if his strategies are diversified enough.

What makes these people algorithmic traders is that they follow strict rules for entry and exit. That is the real key – they are 100% rule followers. With those strict rules, they can historically backtest their approaches, and while "past performance is not indicative of future results" (as a U.S. government disclaimer correctly states), it is very nice to realize that the strategies traded have worked in the past.

Many traders can't commit to 100% rule following, so they fall into the last major category – hybrid trading.

Hybrid Trading

Now that I have discussed discretionary trading, and algorithmic trading, it is time to bring another type of trading into the mix – what I call hybrid trading.

Hybrid trading is simply a mix of discretionary and algo trading. Some examples:

- Entries are based on technical indicators and rules, but exits are left to the discretion of the trader
- Entries are based on trader judgment, but once in a trade, an automated exit "bot" controls the trade, with no trader intervention
- Entries and exits are both well defined by rules, but the trader has discretion to overrule. For example, a trader might decide to ignore long stock signals after a natural or manmade disaster. Or a trader might decide to go flat before major world events (Brexit vote, Trump election night).

The advantage in hybrid trading is that the trader can still have some discretionary influence on the trade. That is also a disadvantage! One thing I have noticed with my own algo trading is that some of my best algo trades turn out to be ones that my "human judgment" absolutely hated! If I treated those trades as hybrid trades, I would have negated all the good effects of the algo.

*****

Reading the last section, you might wonder "what are the professional traders out there doing, and how can I possibly compete with them?" Great question! Pros are using all of the methods detailed above. You can compete by treating trading as a serious endeavor. Don't wish for "I have 15 minutes a day for trading" type systems. Wish for being the best you can be at trading – then you'll be good competition for the pros.

Of all these types of trading, it is hard to decide which trading route is for you. Throughout the book, I'll discuss some of the characteristics and traits that make for good algorithmic traders, but for now I will assume that you already know algo trading is the path you want to pursue. If you still aren't sure, though, keep reading and maybe by the end of the book you will be sure!

CHAPTER 2 - ALGO TRADING BASICS

"I believe rules are meant to be broken." – Film producer Robert Evans (likely NOT a successful trader)

Anytime you trade, whether you are a beginner, intermediate or expert, you are using rules to trade. You might not realize the rules, the rules may change from day to day, or hour to hour, but there are rules. The rule is your decision making process – how you decide whether to enter or exit any particular trade. It might be chaotic and disjointed, but there is a rule somewhere in there. Maybe your rule is "rules are made to be broken!"

So when the goofy talking head on CNBC screams "buy this stock!" and you follow his recommendation?
RULE: Blowhard says buy, you buy.

Your cousin calling you with the hot tip?
RULE: Crazy cousin says he has "inside" info, you buy only if his last tip was profitable.

Using technical indicators?
RULE: If the price is above 20 period average, and the RSI value is below 20, Sell short.

The list is never ending – there are an infinite number of rules to buy and sell. But when they are written down, followed exactly, and not subject to judgment or discretion, then those rules can be transformed into an algorithm.

What Is In A Typical "Algo?"

Let's take a look at the components of a typical trading algorithm. I'll also give some simple examples, in plain English and in Tradestation Easy Language.

Long Entry

This is an absolute requirement – how are you going to enter the market on the long (buy) side? You have to have criteria, or a set of criteria, to enter the market.

An example of this could be a simple momentum type entry:

Pseudo Code: Enter long on the open of the next bar if current closing price is greater than the closing price 5 bars ago.

Tradestation Easy Language Code: if close>close[5] then buy next bar at market;

Short Entry

If you are trading stocks, you may not want to be short the market (https://www.investopedia.com/terms/s/shortselling.asp). But for futures and forex, you almost certainly will want to be able to go short – to benefit from a price decline. In that case, you will want a short entry rule.

Now, this rule could be the exact opposite of the long entry rule, or it could be something completely different. That is the neat thing about creating your own algorithm – you can set it up however you wish. This ability to customize algos to your preferences has a hidden benefit – I have found it much easier to adhere to the rules of a strategy I created, compared to a strategy where someone else dictated the rules. And remember, good algorithmic trading is all about following the rules.

An example of a short entry could be a simple moving average crossover:

Pseudo Code: Enter short on the next bar if the closing prices crosses below the 7 period moving average.

Tradestation Easy Language Code: if close crosses below average(close,7) then sell short next bar at market;

Long Exit

Obviously, if you have a long entry rule, you also need a long exit rule. This exit could be based on the current position's profit or loss (see "stop loss" and "profit target" on the next few pages), or it could be based on a technical indicator, chart pattern, etc. It is just some trigger to tell you to exit the long position.

An example of a long exit could be a chart pattern – exit after 2 consecutive down closes:

Pseudo Code: Exit long position if close of this bar is less than close of previous bar, and close of previous bar is less than close of 2 bars ago.

Tradestation Easy Language Code: if close<close[1] and close[1]<close[2] then sell next bar at market;

Short Exit

If you have a short entry, you will likely want a short exit.

An example of a short exit could to close every Thursday:

Pseudo Code: Exit short if today is Thursday.

Tradestation Easy Language Code: if dayofweek(Date)=4 then buytocover next bar at market;

Stop And Reverse

For the long and short exits above, the current position would be closed, leaving the trader flat. But what if you wanted to reverse the position? Let's say you were long, and if certain criteria is met, you want to exit your long AND go short at the same time?

An example would be to reverse long and go short if a new low was hit:

Pseudo Code: Exit long, and go short, if the current bar low is the lowest low of last 12 bars.

Tradestation Easy Language Code: if low=lowest(low,12) then sellshort next bar at market;

Stop Loss

Most algo traders want to protect themselves in case of an adverse price move. The thinking is that at some point it makes sense to exit the market, regardless of what the technical indicators, chart pattern or whatever entry signal used indicates. That can be achieved by a simple stop loss.

Pseudo Code: Exit position if the loss of the current position hits -$500.

Tradestation Easy Language Code: SetStopLoss(500);

Profit Target

As with the stop loss, most algo traders want to exit if price goes in their favor. When a certain profit level is hit, they want to exit.

Pseudo Code: Exit position if the profit of the current position hits +$2500.

Tradestation Easy Language Code: SetProfitTarget(2500);

Position Sizing

As an optional feature, you may want the algorithm to determine how many shares or contracts to buy/sell. This includes the concept of position sizing, which is a whole topic onto itself! Some common position sizing techniques include fixed fractional and fixed ratio, along with the simple "trade x contracts per $y of equity."

Pseudo Code: Trade 1 contract for every $10,000 in current equity (starting equity plus profits to date)

Tradestation Easy Language Code: ncons = int((startingequity+NetProfit)/10000); buy ncons contracts next bar at market;

Order Types

The types of orders that can be placed by your algorithm depend in part on the trading platform. The three most common types are market orders, stop orders and limit orders.

Tradestation Easy Language Code:

```
//Market order
Buy Next Bar At Market;

//Stop Order
Sell Next Bar at XXXX stop;  //where XXXX=price you want to exit at, below the
current market price

//Limit Order
Sell Next Bar at XXXX limit;  //where XXXX=price you want to exit at, above the
current market price
```

Big Order Fill Algos

All of the algo components I have just mentioned can all be used by retail traders. Large professional traders have their own algos, which you may have heard about. These include various types of "fill" algos – schemes to trade large quantities of an instrument. When you are trading 1000 contracts of something like the mini S&P futures, you can't just submit a market order for 1,000 contracts – it will disrupt the market, and give you a poor average fill price. The order needs to be "worked," that is broken down into small chunks, and fill over a specific time or around a specific price.

You likely will never need these types of algos, but you should be aware that they exist.

Higher Level Algos

In the example components just given, it was assumed that the trader was trading a single algorithm. But what happens when the trader has 10, 20 or more algorithms? How do things work then?

The answer is that once one codes a single algorithm, these algos can stand alone, or they can "talk" to each other. Perhaps you will want to limit the number of open positions arising from different algos, or maybe base your position sizing on profits to date from all algorithms. The possibilities can be mind boggling, and go beyond the scope of this introductory book. But it is worthwhile to understand these "add ons" to a simple one market algorithm exist.

For many traders, to keep things simple, they treat each algo as if it is in its own little world. Then, they use outside analysis (perhaps in Excel) to put the algos in a portfolio, to determine proper risk exposure, proper position sizing, etc. It is an exercise a beginning algo trader will not have to worry about just yet, but should at least be aware of.

Putting It All Together

Here is a simple example of an algo that goes long and short, has a stop loss and profit target, can stop and reverse and also can go flat. It includes a simple position sizing approach, too. I do not recommend it (since you personally have not tested and verified this algo is a money maker), but you could put this in your trading platform and start trading.

Tradestation Easy Language Code:

```
Input: StartingCapital (10000);
Var: Ncons(1);
//position sizing calculation
Ncons=Round(((StartingCapital+NetProfit)/10000),0);

//long and short entries, will stop and reverse
If close>close[5] then buy Ncons contracts next bar at market;
```

If close<close[5] then sellshort Ncons contracts next bar at market;

//long and short technical type exits
If close=lowest(close,3) then sell next bar at market;
If close=highest(close,3) then buytocover next bar at market;

//standard dollar based stop loss and profit target
Setstopcontract;
SetStopLoss(500);
SetProfitTarget(2000);

CHAPTER 3 – IS ALGO TRADING FOR YOU?

"You don't have enough experience."
"You are just not the right person for the job."
"You would not be a good fit for this position / for our organization."

If you have ever looked for a job, chances are you heard one or more of these excuses from a potential employer. The problem is how do you know that what they are saying is true, without even giving you a chance to prove yourself?

Algo trading is the same way, except that eventually you will find out if algo trading is right for you. Unfortunately, though, the way traders find out is by the market extracting money from your account!

I am going to shortcut that painful process for you.

In later chapters, I'll help with the first rejection – experience. This book will help you get the experience you need to start to algo trade. You'll be on the right path, although there will be a lot more to do.

For the other two rejections – knowing if you are the right person for algo trading, and if this type of trading "fits" your personality – in this chapter I'll discuss some of the important personality characteristics and traits I think are important (or not important) to be a successful algo trader.

Remember, you are a small retail trader, and the trading world is full of professional "sharks." If you want to compete, you first have to know if algo trading fits you. This chapter is a great way to find out.

My advice is to get a piece of paper, write down each of the traits I list, and then after I explain it, grade yourself on each one. You'll soon see if algorithmic trading fits you!

Analytical Thinking

Scientists say there are two types of people in the world, left brain thinkers and right brain thinkers. Left brain people tend to be more analytical, numbers oriented. Typically, these people are found in positions like doctors, lawyers, accountants, scientists, engineers, computer programmers, etc. Rules appeal to these sorts of people.

Right brain people, on the other hand, tend to be more free thinkers. Artists, musicians, sales people, marketing folk and other "soft skill" careers tend to be their domain.

Both types of people are important to the world. Think of life without artists like Monet, composers like Beethoven, brilliant logical thinkers like Einstein. The world would be a sad place without a mix.

In trading, certain areas seem to work better for lefties and righties. Right brain traders may be more in tune with visual chart trading, and discretionary trading. Most traders I have worked with for algo trading tend to be more left brain thinkers. Over the years, I have done algo work with many doctors and scientists, but not so many artists.

Now I realize I have really oversimplified things here. But in general, the analytical type left brain thinkers are more likely to find algo trading appealing, and are more likely to succeed at it.

Give yourself one point if you are primarily a left brain, analytical thinker.

Control Freak?

A while back, I met a trader for coffee. He was going to go live with his forex system the next week. He had years of favorable backtests, solid and 100% defined rules, and he had automation all set up.

So, a week later, I asked him how things went. He told me he made $500 that first week, on a $5,000 account. Nice, I told him. But he shook his head and sheepishly replied "Not really. I turned the system on and off a few times during the week. Had I just let it run, I would have made $2,500!"

He was a classic control freak. But he is not that unusual.

Many traders like to have "their finger on the button" – to always be ready to enter or exit a trade at a moment's notice when something does not feel right. The idea of letting a computer alone control entries and exits is anathema to what these people are all about. These traders want, and actually crave, the ultimate control over trades.

A good non-trading example of this is with "helicopter" parents. These are parents who hover over their children, ready to swoop in at a moment's notice to "save" their progeny, no matter their age. I have even heard of these helicopter control freaks e-mailing college professors and employers on behalf of their children! Control freaks, to the max.

Algo trading, on the other hand, is all about letting go. It is about preparing, testing, and setting up the trading strategy, but when the time comes, letting go and letting the backtest proven algorithm do its job. It is not easy to do, especially at first. But it is essential to proper algorithmic trading.

If you are NOT a control freak, give yourself one point.

Tinkerers/Perfectionists

Do you have the need to be right, to be perfect? That is a great attribute to have in school, and also in many "analytical" type careers. But it is awful to have in trading!

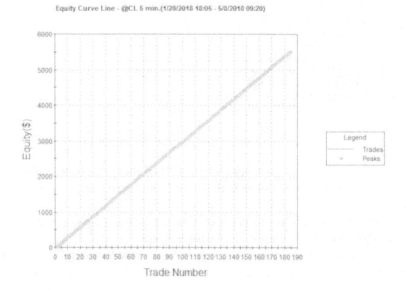

Figure 7- Should This Be Your Goal When Backtesting? (Answer: "No!")

Why? Why shouldn't we, as traders, aim for terrific looking historical backtests, for trading perfection?

The answer might come as a shock – NOOOOO!

Looking for perfection, tinkering with a trading algorithm until it produces a great backtest, is actually about the worst thing you can do. You actually trick yourself, thinking that by continually testing, you make things better (notice a bit of control freakiness in that?).

But the best traders only test as much as they absolutely need to. They realize perfection is impossible, so they do not try to achieve it.

Think of things you do outside trading – if you always strive to be perfect, or always try to improve things, that is an algo trading warning sign. Give yourself 1 point if you are NOT a perfectionist or tinkerer.

Emotionally Charged People

Figure 8- Does This Keg Of Dynamite Describe Your Typical Emotional State? Not Good For A Trader!

Some folks, by nature, are very excitable. They cheer the loudest, they boo the loudest, they wear their hearts on their sleeve. You almost always know where they stand on an issue.

On the other hand, some folks are calm under pressure, never get rattled, never get too high, or too low – regardless of what happens.

Which are you? Give yourself two points if you consider yourself calm, cool and collected most of the time. It is a great way to be when you are algo trading.

Patient People

Take a minute and google the phrase "trading system quick wealth." You'll find over 2,000,000 matches.

Then google "trading system slow wealth" – you will only see about 300,000 matches.

Clearly, most people want wealth quickly – I mean, who really wants to wait? Yet waiting and patience is a big key to success. You are not going to create a dozen algorithms the first week after you start algo trading. And your algos likely will not make you rich overnight.

Good trading is about being patient, letting trades play out, letting strategies play out. Have you ever tried a new strategy, then abandoned it after a week of losing money? Maybe your strategy was indeed a loser, but maybe it just had an unlucky week.

Think of trading like running a long foot race. Many runners start sprinting from the start. Some pull a hamstring because they weren't properly warmed up. Others get off to a big lead, but then they realize – they are in a marathon race of 26.2 miles, not a 100 yard dash!

Treat trading as a marathon. Take your time, be patient. As they say "Rome was not built in one day." Give yourself 1 point if you are able to take things slowly.

Rule Followers

Have you ever seen little kids color in a coloring book? Some will neatly stay within the lines. Others will treat the lines as a guideline only, and draw whatever the heck they want. Both can create beautiful final masterpieces though!

Figure 9 - How Do You Color?

Earlier, I spoke about left brain and right brain people. I would guess that rule followers tend to be more left brain oriented, but not always.

Good algo traders tend to be rule followers. Give yourself one point if you consider yourself a rule follower.

Frequently Frustrated Folk

I have three kids, all pretty much equally talented. But when it comes to sports, many times my youngest comes up short. The problem? He gets easily frustrated.

As soon as a roadblock appears in his way, he gives up, or pouts, gets mad and then gives up.

He'd be a terrible algo trader, at least right now.

How "frustration free" are you? Developing algo strategies is chock full of frustration. If you cannot handle setbacks, roadblocks and near constant frustration, you will be in trouble. Algo trading system development is not easy – if it was everyone would do it!

Give yourself two points if you can handle and overcome frustration easily.

Process Oriented Practitioners

How do you currently evaluate potential strategies? Do you evaluate each one the same, running through the same steps? If so, give yourself one point – following a defined process is good for algo traders.

If you don't have a process, whether that be for finding and testing trading strategies, actual trading or analysis of your trading results after the fact, give yourself zero points.

The best algo traders tend to be the most process oriented. They consistently adhere to their approach to the markets, and in how they go about trading.

Why is this important? Simply put, there is no right way to trade, but there are a million wrong ways. By being a consistent, process oriented trader, one can more easily make in-course adjustments.

In the field of Quality Assurance, it is known as the Plan Do Check Act cycle. In the Act phase, a trader will figure out ways to improve upon what he or she is doing. Imagine how hard it is to make changes when there is no set process! (Hint: it is really impossible. Having a process lends itself to making improvements).

PLAN NEW PROJECT

EXECUTE PLAN

IMPROVEMENT ACTIONS

ANALYSE DATA

Figure 10- Plan Do Check Act Quality Improvement Tool

Add one point to your total if you are process oriented.

Grand Total

How did you do? There were 10 possible points with this exercise.

- If you hit 9 or 10 points, congrats! You have most of the skills and traits necessary to conquer algo trading.
- If you hit 6-8 points, you are close to being algo ready, but you are not quite there yet. Take some time, and work on the areas where you fall short.
- If you scored 5 or fewer points, take a step back and re-evaluate your situation. Is algo trading really what you want to do? It is not for everyone, and certainly, it is better to find out now that your personality does not mesh with algo trading, rather than down the road, after a lot of likely wasted time and wasted money. Algo trading is not for everyone, so if your personality does not support it, I recommend you look at a different type of trading.

The Good News

The good news is if you are really excited about the possibilities of algo trading, with a little effort you can turn each of your liabilities into an asset. For example, if you do not have a set process for trading, go create one, and most importantly, follow it. If you get easily frustrated, or you are an emotional powder keg, realizing that is the first step to changing it. It will take some time, but before you even think about algo trading, spend some time working on yourself. Once you can score 9 or 10 on the exercise, then you'll be in good shape to start taking part in the many advantages of algorithmic trading.

By Kevin J. Davey

CHAPTER 4 – THE MANY ADVANTAGES OF ALGO TRADING

A t this point, you hopefully have a decent idea on what algo trading is, and what it isn't. But you still may be wondering "why should I algo trade?" This chapter will discuss the many advantages for retail algo traders.

Advantage #1 – No Charlatans With Questionable Trades

A few years ago, I sat in on the webinar of an alleged "trading guru." This person – I won't even call him a trader, since I highly doubt he even actively traded – was a so called expert on trendline trading.

Trendline trading, for those of you unfamiliar with the term, is a method where you draw lines on price charts to capture the major trends. Special significance is given to times where the price touches a trendline and bounces off it, and also to times where the price touches the trendline and then keeps on going through it. In the first instance, the trendline is supposedly "respected" and in the second case, the trendline is "rejected." Both are purportedly meaningful.

This is not the time or place to talk about the validity of such an approach – maybe randomly drawn lines would also sometimes show significance – but the point it is a trading method out there the many people use. Most people using trendlines are likely discretionary traders, where the trendline is just one of the factors (including trader judgment) that influence trade signals. They have rules, but sometimes the rules are fuzzy – not suitable for algo trading.

Anyhow, at one point in the webinar, the presenter showed the following chart:

Figure 11- Trendline "Guru" Trade

"Just look at this example," the carnival barking presenter exclaimed, "This shows the greatness and perfection of trendline trading! A perfect entry, a perfect exit, no danger of a stop being hit, lots of profit. Truly a great trade! Follow my teachings and I'll show you many, many more of these."

No doubt, on the surface, this seems like a great trade. And most of the people in that room were fooled by it, likely plunking down thousands of dollars for "trendline secrets."

But the alleged guru was actually a charlatan. A charlatan showing fantastical, fake trades. How can I say this? Well, let's look a little deeper at this "trade."

First, this trade – if you can even call it that – is purely the result of hindsight bias. This occurs from looking at a completed chart, and then going back and picking a great looking trade. It is easy to do, and hard to "unsee" once you've done it.

Just look at the entry. It is almost at the upper trend line, and based on that it looks valid. But how could that upper trendline have even been drawn? A few bars before the alleged entry, a proper trendline would have looked like the line in red, not the line in blue. There was no way to draw the blue upper trendline until AFTER the entry occurred. How are you supposed to trade that way? (Answer: you can't!)

How do you draw the upper TL in blue, BEFORE the entry supposedly occurs?

Data is Indicative

Figure 12- Hindsight Bias Makes For Great Looking Trendlines!

That is the charlatan's first sleight of hand – using hindsight bias.

But the shenanigans of this pretend trader do not stop there. Let's assume for a second that the improperly drawn hindsight bias trendline was correct, and take a closer look at the entry. Note how the price does not even touch the trendline at the entry point. In other words a phantom entry! How close does the price have to be to the trendline to count as an entry?

Phantom Entry

Figure 13- A "Close Enough" Entry

So mistake #2 is assuming a "close enough" entry is valid – you can't do that with a computer tested algo!

Of course, since the guru cheated on the trendline, and gave a phantom entry, is there any reason to believe he got the exit right? Take a look...

Price never even touches incorrect TL, let alone correct TL!

Figure 14- Incorrect Lower Trendline Changes The Exit Point!

31

No surprise here – the guru drew the lower trendline incorrectly, which made the trade appear profitable. But when the trendline is drawn correctly (shown in red in figure above), the profit target NEVER gets hit!

That is the charlatan's third sleight of hand – drawing an incorrect trendline to fake a profitable exit.

So, the charlatan's perfect trade was anything but. Bad trendlines, bad entry and bad exit. In other words, a complete farce of a trade.

Why is this important to algo trading? In algo trading, the rules are programmed, and can be accurately tested. No phantom trades, no "close enough" scenarios. The rules in an algo strategy are clear, and the results are unambiguous. The Performance Report can be brutal in its truthfulness, and it does not lie.

Most trading education charlatans (and there are a ton of them) hate algo trading for just this reason. When their supposed awesome techniques are put to a proper test, their approach usually fails miserably.

Advantage #2 – Increased Confidence Through Backtesting

Just as charlatan approaches are revealed through proper testing, historical backtesting can help you immensely with your strategies. This is a HUGE advantage. Think about the options you have before deciding to trade a particular strategy:

A. Trading a strategy where someone else told you "this strategy is great"
B. Trading a strategy you have not tested that you think might be profitable
C. Trading a strategy you have tested and found to lose money historically
D. Trading a strategy you have tested and determined has made money historically

This might seem like an easy question to answer, and it might even seem ridiculous to you that I even ask it. But, in the real world, you would be amazed at how many people pick the first three options! Let's take a look:

A. Trading a strategy where someone else told you "this strategy is great"

This is the most common approach to trading. Some guru will tell you how great his or her strategy is, and may even show some hypothetical equity curves to prove it. The strategy could be from a book or a magazine. Or, maybe the strategy itself is kept secret, with resulting signals provided in a chat or trade room.

As far as strategies you might see in a book or a trading magazine, before you trade it, realize that the results shown will ALWAYS be good. Think about it for a second – would you buy a magazine which reveals a trading strategy that lost money? Of course not. So magazine article authors will do everything they can to show profitable results for their strategy. Unfortunately, that usually leads to poor real time performance, since their strategy was developed based on false pretenses.

The end result with this option is that many people rely on someone else to have done the dirty work – the testing. The question then becomes "Are you willing to risk your hard earned money based on the word of another person?"

B. Trading a strategy you have not tested that you think might be profitable

This sounds crazy – trading a strategy where you really have no idea if it is profitable or not. An example would be buying any stock that hits a 52 week high, on the theory that it is moving up. This is a reasonable theory, but who knows? Shouldn't you test it first?

C. Trading a strategy you have tested and found to lose money historically

With the third option, we are getting closer to something good. You take a strategy, and then test it on historical data, to see if it works. That is good. Unfortunately, what many people do is first they see unprofitable results, and second they ignore the results. That sounds crazy, but many people have a "pet" idea, and they are determined that it is valid, regardless of what a historical backtest might say.

D. Trading a strategy you have tested and determined has made money historically

This final option is the only truly sensible option, and it is what you want to do with your algos. You create an algo, program it in your trading platform (you could also program and test by hand, but it is laborious), and then test it on historical data (backtest it). If it is profitable, you consider trading it. If it is not profitable, you simple discard the strategy, and create another, different, strategy.

The theory here is that if a strategy worked in the past, it is more likely to work in the future. Note I said "more likely." It is far from a guarantee of future performance. It could be that the market could change somehow, or that you made mistakes during the historical test, and that the future performance of the strategy might be terrible.

But all things being equal, don't you think it is best to at least have a strategy that you have verified has performed well in the past, compared to the other options? That is a major advantage to algo trading – the ability to test. Knowing a strategy was properly tested with profitable results gives you a lot of confidence when you start live trading. None of the options A-C above can give you that type of assurance.

Advantage #3 – Diversification

There is no "Holy Grail" in trading. There is no strategy or algorithm that will work forever, generating profits consistently with little or no drawdown. Most professional traders know this.

But, diversification comes close to the Holy Grail, at least closer than anything else I have ever seen in my 25+ years of trading.

Why is diversification an advantage with algo trading? The answer is volume. With algo trading, once you have a solid development process established – one that produces profitable trading strategies – you simply create more and more strategies, creating a large library of strategies.

There are two keys when you do this, both related. First, you will diversify by markets. With futures, for examples, there are approximately 40 different markets to choose from in the US. These are broadly grouped into 6 different sectors:

Stock Market Indices
Agricultural Products and Softs
Currencies
Precious Metals
Interest Rates
Energies

By creating multiple strategies in multiple markets, you create a diversified portfolio. Maybe one week currency strategies will not work well, for instance, but that could be offset by good performance in metals or energies.

The second key is to create different types of algorithms, for different market regimes and behaviors. You will create trend following algos, and also counter trend (mean reverting) strategies. These tend to balance each other out over time.

To be successful with multiple algorithms, in different markets and with different trading styles, one requirement is paramount: the strategy results should have low correlation with each other. It does little good to have a gold algorithm that has up and down periods at the exact same times as a crude oil strategy. That high amount of correlation would increase, rather than decrease, your portfolio risk.

The reason diversification works is, with uncorrelated algorithms, drawdowns and rough patches occur at different times for different strategies. Maybe a Euro strategy is in a drawdown, but at the same time a Soybean strategy is hitting new equity highs. This is shown in the figure below, where as more and more algorithmic strategies are added, the cumulative equity curve becomes steeper, and the equity curve gets smoother.

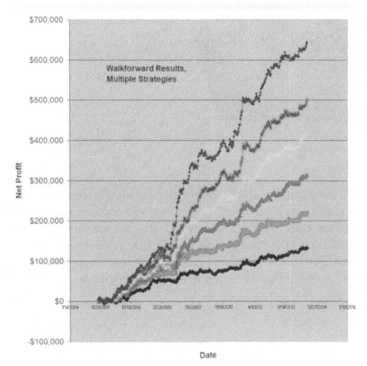

Figure 15 - With Multiple Uncorrelated Strategies, Profits Add, But Drawdowns Do Not

With the help of trading software, diversification is fairly easy with algorithms. Since they can be automated, it is not difficult for trading software to monitor 10, 20 or even 100's of trading strategies, entering and exits according to each strategies' own rules. That can become a major advantage.

Advantage #4 – No Computer Vision Syndrome

If you have been around for a while, I'm sure you've heard about the "screen zombies" – traders who are glued to their computer screen during stock market hours, or maybe all night for Japanese or European hours. These people don't lose focus of the emerging price patterns, even forgoing eating and bathroom breaks.

Figure 16 - Is This How You Want To Trade?

That doesn't sound like too much fun for me. But, I guess if it works for them...

Algo trading is completely different. Sure, you will still spend time at the computer, testing new ideas, monitoring positions, etc. But algo trading does not require constant viewing of a trading screen. In fact, given human nature to overrule algorithms, staring at a screen while algo trading is not even desired.

The freedom from the computer screen that algo trading gives you is a major advantage.

Advantage #5 – Total Control

When you create and trade algorithms, you are in control. You decide all of the following:

- ✓ What markets to trade
- ✓ What types of algos to trade
- ✓ Specifics performance characteristics of each algo (profit, drawdown, expectancy, etc)
- ✓ How and when to turn algos on and off
- ✓ Position sizing each algo, in a portfolio
- ✓ When you will be in trades, when you will not (weekends, overnight)

The list above is not even complete, but you get the idea. You can pick and choose the characteristics of what you are trading, and how you are trading. No more relying on anyone else for black box strategies, signals, etc.

This feeling of control becomes important during the inevitable down periods. Why? Consider two traders:

- Trader A trades a black box strategy. He has no idea what goes into it. It could include random guessing, for all he knows. Sometimes, he has seen it take trades that he disagrees with. It starts to go into a drawdown.
- Trader B trades an algorithm he created. He knows how the strategy was created, knows when it will likely trade, and also knows how long it will likely take to recover. It also starts to go into a drawdown.

Most traders, when given a choice, would undoubtedly prefer to be Trader B. The more you know about an algorithm, and how it was developed, the more comfort you will have, because of the confidence you have in the algorithm construction. It is difficult to be confident of an algorithm where most of its important characteristics are secret.

Of course, all this freedom can be overwhelming, especially to a trader brand new to algo trading. But all these features do not have to be addressed from the start. Starting off with trading one or two algorithms, with one contract each (or a small share size in the case of stocks), is a great way to "dip your toes in the water" of algo trading, without being overwhelmed. Then, as time goes on, and profits (hopefully) accumulate, a trader can start to explore the advanced topics the come with portfolio trading.

Control over your trading, then, is a major advantage to algo trading.

Advantage #6 – Always Ready and Willing To Work

Imagine that you are a business owner, running a fast food franchise. To be successful, you need employees. Some of your employees are great, and you are lucky to have them working for your business.

But other employees mainly cause problems. They show up late for work, they steal from you, they insult your customers. Sometimes you wonder "do I really need all this hassle?"

The human factor can be a big factor in the success of your business. Not so with trading algorithms, though.

Your algorithms are your workers. They do what they are told. They do not take off for sick time. They can work 24 hours a day, 6 days a week – whenever the markets are open. They are always ready to go. They do not get scared in volatile markets. They do not get bored and miss trades in flat markets.

Sure, some algos will "steal" from you, causing you to lose money, but for the most part, the algorithms are reliable, loyal employees. Your job will be to pick the right ones!

*****

After reading through these major advantages, hopefully you can see why algos appeal to so many traders. You might, in fact, be ready to jump in right now and start trading algos. Not so fast, though – read the next chapter first.

CHAPTER 5 – THE DISADVANTAGES AND MISCONCEPTIONS OF ALGO TRADING

After reading the previous chapter, the world of algo trading might seem to be a nirvana, compared to your current method of trading. Unfortunately, it is anything but. Algo trading, like any type of trading, is extremely tough and full of pitfalls. It is important that you realize some of the major disadvantages before you embark on your algorithmic trading career. These disadvantages might just change your mind about wanting to algo trade.

Disadvantage #1 – Emotions Are Still A Part Of Trading

I still vividly remember my first "algo" trade, the same one I talk about in the introduction. No one called it algorithmic trading back then, but that is what it was. I had rules, I followed the rules, and I should have been emotionless, like a robot.

Instead, I was scared to death!

I called the broker every 15 minutes and asked "can I get the last price for June Live Hogs?" Then I'd calculate my open position profit or loss based on the latest number. For the next 15 minutes, I'd either be euphoric because I was making money, or depressed because I was losing money. The broker started getting annoyed with my constant calls. There was no online way to check prices then, if you recall those olden days. If there would have been online quotes, I'm sure I would have refreshed that quote page every minute.

So why was I scared to death, acting like a crazy person? After all, so many people say that when you trade with rules, it takes the emotion out of trading. I should have been a calm, cool, collected robot.

Except I wasn't – I was a bundle of stomach wrenching nerves!

The truth is that ANY time you are trading with money, emotions enter into the equation. The rapid gain or loss of capital is what brings on the emotion, not the style of trading. Algo trading, discretionary trading, random guessing trading – it does not matter which approach you take- is emotional once money is involved.

So, how come so many "gurus" out there recommend algo trading because it is supposedly emotionless? I believe it is all a sales ploy by these crooks. The charlatans know that emotions ruin a lot of traders, and that traders are looking to avoid emotion, so they claim that algo trading solves the emotion problem.

Except it doesn't. As I said, emotions are because of the money involved, not the type of trading. My personal guess is that people who say algo trading is emotionless either 1) trade only on a simulator, or 2) do not trade at all, in any fashion. They clearly do not trade with real money.

That being said, the emotions experienced by algo trading are a bit different than the emotions of discretionary trading. Gone is the panic feeling of wondering if you should enter or exit a trade. But, that is replaced with the panic feeling of wondering if you should turn an algo on or off. Basically, for every event in discretionary trading that causes emotion, there is likely a similar, but different, parallel emotion in algo trading.

So the first misconception in algo trading – that there is no emotion - is also the first disadvantage. Trading with real money involves emotion. You must learn to accept that.

Disadvantage #2 – Computer Programming

If the thought of having to program a computer scares you, then maybe algo trading is not for you. Although there are visual programming tools out there to assist, to really be a good algo trader, you need to be able to program your trading rules. True, you could just hire someone to do that for you, but since most algos fail testing, paying someone to program will get expensive very quickly. Programming thousands of algos is a big task.

So, if you decide to algo, just convince yourself right now that you will learn to program. Once you start doing it, knowing how to program will move this from a disadvantage to an advantage.

Disadvantage #3 – The Past Is Not The Future

If you have seen ads for trading education, trading systems, brokers, etc. you have undoubtedly seen the U.S. government required disclaimer "past performance is not necessarily indicative of future results."

This is a great warning for all traders. It simply means that no matter what historical testing shows, it does not mean the performance will continue in the future. In fact, many times the opposite happens, sort of a reversion to the mean situation.

This presents a conundrum for algo traders, who almost always historically backtest their approaches before commencing with live trading. Why even backtest if the past performance doesn't correlate with future performance?

Obviously, backtesting an algo presents a sticky situation. A trader wants the reassurance that an algo did work historically, and yet at the same time must realize that everything could fall apart from day one of live trading.

The trick, it turns out, is to have a development method that has been proven to work in historical testing and real time testing. It is not as simple as just optimizing parameters, as most trading platforms would make you believe. This will be discussed in more detail later.

Historical testing, then, is like walking a tightrope over a pit of molten lava. Once false move, and death awaits. But when done correctly, the crowd cheers in awe. Our goal will obviously be the latter result!

Disadvantage #4 – Tweaking Is Fun

When I first drafted the book, one female proof reader asked me "why is twerking a disadvantage? Twerking is fun, and I love to do it, but I don't get what it has to do with trading."

Well, that might be true, although I am a little too old to be twerking (trust me!). And besides, the word is TWEAKING. Changing one letter makes a big difference!

Tweaking is the natural tendency to want to change and improve things. As I showed earlier, making improvements is an important part of trading. But, it is not a desired part of algo development. Tweaking can really cause problems.

Here is an example: I have a trader friend who has been developing and tweaking his strategy for over 5 years. Every time he has a losing trade, he examines it closely, and finds a reason why that trade was invalid. He then creates a rule – a tweak – to eliminate that trade. His backtest looks better, since that pesky trade will never occur again, and he is happy.

Happy, of course, until the next tweak is needed.

So, for over five years, his strategy has been tweaked to death. In fact, I'd wager that his algo has much more tweaking code than original strategy code. And, unfortunately, his real time results never get better. There is always one more tweak to be done.

Tweaking your code is easy. But it is wrong to do, and that makes it a big disadvantage for algo trading.

Disadvantage #5 – I'm The Boss Here!

Earlier, I wrote about having a business with employees. With trading, the only employee is typically yourself. This can be a major advantage – no employees to coddle or stress over – but it can also be a major disadvantage.

If your algo strategies fail to perform – it is usually your fault.

If you fail to develop new strategies – only you are to blame.

If you make mistakes in automating your algos, perform futures contract rollovers incorrectly, miss deadlines – it falls on you.

No matter what the decision, or what the action, for better or worse, you are the Big Cheese, the Head Honcho, the Top Dog (https://www.youtube.com/watch?v=0yC4gm_vN3s).

While this might seem to be the ultimate freedom for people stuck in jobs they do not like, working for bosses they hate, the truth is that it can be a major disadvantage, too.

In algo trading, when things falls apart – and they will, at least temporarily, to some extent and to some degree – there is no one to blame but yourself. Many traders cannot handle that kind of pressure and accountability.

Being the boss can be great, especially with algo trading. But, just remember that it can also be a big disadvantage.

Disadvantage #6 – Doing Things The Wrong Way

Algo trading, when done the right way, can work out very well. The problem is that it is exceedingly easy to algo trade incorrectly. And guess what, the wrong way usually leads to losses.

This is a major disadvantage for algo trading because there are many, many ways to develop a trading strategy incorrectly. The list is so long, in fact, that I could probably write a whole book on how NOT to develop trading algo – and maybe one day I will! Many biases, shown below, can really mess up your algo trading.

Figure 17- Each One Of These Biases Can Lead To Improper Algo Development

So, with all these algo development pitfalls, how can a trader turn this from a disadvantage to an advantage? Surely, if most traders make mistakes during algo creation, then the benefit of correct development becomes even more apparent.

Here are a couple of tips to negate this disadvantage. First, only use trusted sources for your trading advice. The internet is chock full of advice givers, but many of these people do not even trade! Take your advice from someone you know trades.

Second, be willing to take information from many different traders and combine it into something that feels right to you.

Third, prove it via real money trading. Theory is nice, ideas are nicer, but the only thing that matters in the end is the bottom line result. Does your method of algo development produce profits? If it does, congratulations! If it doesn't, you might consider a deep review of your process, and incorporating new concepts or improvements.

Building and trading algos is tough, and there is no one "correct" way to do it. Plus, there are a ton of incorrect ways to do it. That makes this a disadvantage to algo trading.

Disadvantage #7 – Algo Trading Is Not "Set And Forget"

You might recall a number of years ago a portable cooker that was sold on late night television infomercials. Its slogan was "set it and forget it." It was so easy to use, you could just throw food in it, hit a few buttons, and come back a few hours later to a delicious home cooked meal.

Figure 18- Definitely Not The Way To Algo Trade!

Many traders think the same slogan applies to algo trading, especially when automating systems. They are wrong!

Technical support people at Tradestation, a leading trading software platform (and my primary software for trading) have a different slogan: "automated trading does not mean unattended trading."

Whenever you have an automated algo, a million things could go wrong. Internet connections go out, disconnections to trading servers occur, exchanges experience intermittent hiccups, price data corrections come out (but not before the bad data hits your algo) – the list of potential issues is practically infinite.

Multiply all those issues by the dozens of algorithms you might be trading, and the potential for problems becomes very apparent.

You can't turn on an algo, walk away, and come back a week later to count your profits. It just does not work that way. You don't have to be staring at a screen all day and night, making sure your algos are running correctly, but you do have to monitor your algos, at a minimum of a few times per day. You have to be ready to take action when something goes awry. I guarantee you that some intervention will be required more often than you think.

That is the final misconception and disadvantage of algo trading – you have to stay on top of your algos, and keep a watchful eye over them. Definitely do not "set it and forget it!"

CHAPTER 6 – HOW TO BEGIN ALGO TRADING ON YOUR OWN

Since you have read this far, I offer you my congratulations. You already know more about algo trading than probably 90% of people out there. You have learned what it is, what it looks like and what kind of personalities are best suited for it.

You have also been exposed to the advantages and disadvantages of this style of trading, and hopefully the downside has not scared you away. Algo trading can be a fun and rewarding experience, but it is not easy. But as I always say, sometimes the best things in life are the hardest things to do. If algo trading was easy, everyone would do it, and there would be no longer be any financial incentive.

Algo trading can definitely help you compete with the "big boys," but it is not automatically a "supertrader" creator. There is no easy way to trade, and algo trading is no exception. Rest assured there are retail algo traders out there surviving against the hedge funds, commodity trading advisors, etc.

At this point, it is time to set aside theory and words, and get down to business: the business of actually starting to algo trade. The next 3 chapters in this book will get you started:

- Beginning Algo Trading On Your Own
- Selecting A Trading Platform
- Info On Popular Platforms

Following that, I'll give you a simple algo example, followed by tips for successful trading, and finishing up with recommended steps to take after reading this book. When you put it all together, you'll be in a good position to seriously implement algo trading for yourself.

So, let's get started!

What Is The Best Way To Test?

Last year, I met a trader from Atlanta, Georgia in the US. Based on our discussions, I knew he was a knowledgeable trader. Of course, I did not know for sure if he was a profitable trader (who ever knows for sure, unless you see verified trading records?), but it seemed like he was. In any event, I wanted to pick his brain a bit, as I do with many traders I talk to.

I asked this trader "how do you historically backtest?" His reply shocked me. "I don't believe in backtesting," he explained, "since there are so many ways to cheat. I find historical backtesting useless. So, I do not do it, ever." I was flabbergasted. How can someone trade a strategy without at least testing it first, to see if it even produces a profit?

Apparently, this trader saw no need for historical testing, and as crazy as I personally think it is, to each his own, I suppose. I'll assume, though, that you want to historically test your trading algorithms, which is the exact approach I use. How do you do it?

There are four major ways to test a strategy. I'll highlight the pros and cons of each method, before settling on what I think it the best long term solution for a new algo trader. Any of the methods I discuss, though, could work well.

Perform Manual Testing

Even in this digital age of computers, many people are scared of computers. While increased knowledge of computers usually makes them less intimidating, let's assume that some people just do not want to test their trading algorithm with a computer. How can they do it?

The answer brings me back to my early days of trading, where I wrote closing prices on a piece of paper, and calculated moving average with a simple handheld calculator. So I know it can be done.

Manual testing involves the trader looking at each bar, making calculations by hand, and manually recording trades as the algorithm he or she is testing gives signals. If that sounds like a slow and painful process, then I have described it well. Manual testing is slow, cumbersome and very prone to errors.

Do you remember earlier when we saw the trendline trader with his "phantom" trades? Someone manually testing might very well count that as a profitable trade.

"Close enough" is employed by many a manual tester, especially when profits are involved. It is just human nature – to always look for the optimistic outcome for a trade. The issue is that those optimistic backtest trades usually do not pan out in real time trading.

Manual Testing – Pros
- Trader gets an intimate feel for their algo strategy
- Trader feels confident in results, since he meticulously created them

Manual Testing – Cons
- Very time consuming
- Prone to errors
- Extremely easy to cheat, miss bad trades, accept "close enough" trades
- Easy to jump from strategy to strategy after a short test period, instead of testing each strategy the same (no consistency)

Verdict: Not Recommended, unless you only have one strategy to test – ever!

Hire a Programmer/Tester

Probably once a week, I get an e-mail from an aspiring trader. Full of excitement, they want me to program and test their "Holy Grail" trading strategy. Unfortunately, though, they lack the programming skills to do themselves, but they'd be willing to let me trade their creation for free if I just program and test it, again for free.

I always decline, since I know the probable outcome. The strategy probably will not backtest well, and then endless tweaks (remember how bad they are?) and modifications are attempted in a desperate attempt to salvage the alleged Holy Grail. When that fails, new strategies are proposed for programming, and the cycle repeats.

This is why hiring a programmer or tester is usually bad. Programmers are expensive, and if you are serious about algo trading, you will have dozens, if not hundreds, of strategies to program and test. The bill for this effort will be substantial.

The benefit to going this route is that if your strategy is complicated, and your programming skills are weak, a good programmer can finish the job a lot more quickly and efficiently than you ever could. And chances are, with an experienced tester, the results will be believable.

Hiring Programmer/Tester – Pros
- Quality work

- Likely faster than doing it yourself

Hiring Programmer/Tester – Cons

- Large budget needed to program lots of strategies
- Your time required to provide detail work requirements to programmer and tester
- Tendency for simple changes to workscope usually leads to drastically increased costs
- No guarantee what is produced will be useful
- Most programmers and testers are not traders, so the end product may look good, but might also be untradeable

Verdict: Recommended only if you do not have time to program and test on your own, and if you have plenty of money to spend on a programmer

Create Your Own Backtester

Back in the early home computer days, I bought a laptop that I used for work during the day, and trading system evaluation at night. Being on a shoestring budget, I could not afford the premier testing software from Omega Research (later renamed Tradestation). So, since I had some programming knowledge in Fortran and Visual Basic, and advanced knowledge of spreadsheets (Microsoft Excel, Lotus 1-2-3 and Borland Quattro Pro), I decided to create my own backtesting program.

As the months went by, I found that I had a pretty neat little backtest test package. I kept adding on features to make testing go faster, to automate testing, to simulate real conditions, etc. But as the software kept growing, I realized I did not have any finished algos I could trade!

That was a problem, obviously. Somewhere along the line my goal became developing a great backtesting program, instead of developing some trading algorithms.

That is the trap you'll run into if you try to develop your own backtester. Sure, it will be customized to your requirements, but you'll also spend a ton of time working on the software itself, rather than developing strategies. That is true even for advanced programming languages like Python or R. Many open source modules are available in these software languages, giving you a big head start, but you will still spend a lot of time integrating, testing and modifying the pieces.

For a person who is more interested in writing test software, and less so in developing algos, this is a good route to take.

Develop Your Own Backtester – Pros

- You control the look, feel and functionality

- You can trust the results, since you know the programming code intimately (assuming you programmed things correctly, of course!)
- You may be able to test ideas that many retail platforms struggle with (spread trading, options)

Develop Your Own Backtester – Cons
- You need to have programming expertise
- You need trading expertise, so your test engine replicates the real world
- Easy for the software development itself, not trading, to become focus
- Time consuming

Verdict: Recommended for hardcore programmers who want a custom trading solution

Use Retail Trading Software

The final alternative is probably the best one for most retail traders. In today's market, there are literally dozens of trading software packages designed for the retail trader. All have pros and cons, obviously, but the best of them allow traders with little programming knowledge to successfully develop their own trading algorithms.

The great thing about the retail software option is that once you know how to operate the software, and do some simple strategy programming, your focus can be on developing algorithms – exactly where it should be.

Retail Trading Software – Pros
- Most platforms are easy to use and learn
- Used and debugged by other traders, so you can trust results
- Relatively inexpensive, some platforms are even free
- Easy to share strategies with other traders using same software

Retail Trading Software – Cons
- Easy to trick most packages into giving false results
- With so many choices, hard to pick "right" platform
- If software company goes out of business, algos might be useless

Verdict: Recommended for most retail traders. The available software is just too powerful and convenient to disregard.

In case you are wondering, I started out my trading career with the first option, manual backtesting. What a pain! As soon as I had access to a personal computer at night, outside of my regular career working hours, I switched to option 3 – building my own backtesting platform. I did that for a number of years, and had more success in programming the platform than I did in building the algorithms.

I had a few decent algos – or so I thought – but after talking to some more experienced traders, I realized there were issues with my bespoke platform that I was not accounting for properly (for example, some of the intricacies of rollovers). I realized I had to make a drastic change.

Eventually, I decided to go the retail platform route, and I got a copy of Tradestation. I was very scared and intimidated at first by the package (for example, for years I trusted only "buy/sell next bar at market" orders), but eventually I came to understand and felt comfortable with strategy development. And guess what? The algo strategies I started to build became a lot better!

Today, I have been using Tradestation for over 10 years. And baring some unforeseen circumstances, I see myself using it for years to come.

CHAPTER 7 – SELECTING A TRADING SOFTWARE PLATFORM

Back when I started using a retail trading platform (Tradestation), there really weren't too many choices out there. And Tradestation was far and away the best; it had the most features, its backtesting was the most accurate, support was superb and its user group was active and helpful.

Fast forward to today, and the retail software platform landscape is a bit different. Now, there are dozens of trading platforms, and most are pretty good. Each one has some specific "niche" areas it tries to address, usually areas that Tradestation was traditionally not as good at. Of course, Tradestation has responded, and is continually building a better platform. The competition is raising the standard for all platforms, which is tremendous.

This is all great for the retail trader – more competition, better features, lower costs – but it can be overwhelming! Which platform is the best? Which platform has the features you are looking for? Which platform is the easiest to build with? The list of questions goes on and on.

So, I'm not going to try to tell you which platform to use in this chapter, but I will identify some "must haves" that you want for algo trading. In the next chapter, I'll also tell you the most popular platforms, based on trader surveys I have done of the past few years. You might think popularity is a poor criteria to use, but I think it is important. You want a trading platform that will be around for years and years, since transferring your algos from a defunct platform will be cumbersome.

Finally, I'll give you contact information for some of the major platforms, so you can begin to investigate them yourself. It is a personal choice, and you want to feel comfortable with the software you choose, because you will be spending a lot of time with your software choice, building algos!

Charting Capabilities

Theoretically, a pure algo trader and developer does not need price charts of any type. After all, why would that be necessary? Algo rules are what counts, not how things look on a chart. While this is true, a platform with a good charting platform is really good to have.

Many times, during the idea creation phase, an algo trader will want to see his or her idea – an indicator, histogram, bar patterns, whatever – in action. A good charting module in the software will help with that.

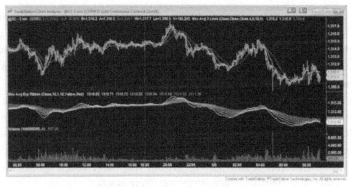

Figure 19 - Charts Can Help You Visualize Aspects Of Your Algorithms

The key with properly using charting is NOT to make any judgments or decisions based on what you see in the chart. Chances are, you are only seeing a small snippet of time on the chart, and the small piece of time can be highly misleading. So concluding that a new indicator or chart pattern is bad, based on a visual examination, is really a terrible thing to do.

On the other hand, using a chart to visually check for correct coding is a great thing to do. A complicated chart pattern might be easy to see, but hard to program algorithmically, so verifying the code by inspecting a chart can be really helpful.

I would recommend good charting capabilities as a definite "must have" for any trading platform.

Broker Integration

Some retail platforms, such as Tradestation, are tied directly to one brokerage (in this case, Tradestation Brokerage). Other platforms, such as NinjaTrader, have a few limited choices in brokers. Finally, some platforms (like Multicharts) have a huge selection of brokers to choose from. There are pros and cons to each approach.

So, searching for a trading platform might also be a search for the proper broker. Personally, I have used many brokers over the years, and two times I've had solid, reputable brokers try to steal my money (Refco, PFG). This means you should be careful with whatever broker you choose, because many can, and do, go out of business.

In all cases, have a backup plan and backup brokers in place, ready to go.

Ease of Programming

Most good platforms offer you the ability to create your own indicators, strategies, etc. – in addition to providing standard indicators with parameters you can change and optimize. If you cannot create your own indicators, I suggest you look elsewhere for a package, since you will definitely be programming your own creations at some point.

Assuming your software allows custom work, there are three main ways to produce custom code. The first way is take existing code, and just modify it to meet your specifications. Once you understand the basics of the programming language, this is pretty easy. I have trader friends who do nothing but this – they have never programmed an original strategy in their career, but they have taken thousands of strategies from others and modified the code to suit their needs.

The second way to produce custom algo code is to start from scratch. This involves a bit more work, but once you get the hang of programming, it is fairly easy to do.

A final way to program code is offered by some platforms, and that is a visual drag and drop code creation approach. You basically move blocks for indicators, patterns, if...then logic, stop losses and more and connect the blocks. Once you are done, the software then turns your visual depiction into code. This is a way around the line by line programming of strategies, but even so, it still involves quite a bit of learning to get up to speed.

It is up to you to decide which approach appeals the most to you. Of course, to make your decision even tougher, each programming language has its own style and format. Some are built off of "professional" heavy duty programming languages like C#, and some of them are built off of "old time" languages like Basic. So programming even a simple strategy can be very easy, or very complicated, depending on the language used.

One way to investigate some different platforms and see different programming languages is to pick up a recent copy of the magazine *"Technical Analysis of Stocks and Commodities."* Almost every month, the editors pick one article (with a new indicator, algo strategy, etc) and have experts from major software platforms create code in their language. This can be found in the "Trader's Tips" section in the back of the magazine.

Figure 20- *"Technical Analysis Of Stocks and Commodities" Magazine "Trader' Tips" Section - A Great Way To Compare Various Programming Languages*

In a recent issue, 11 different trading platforms provided code for a new RSI indicator produced by John Ehlers, a well-respected developer. By taking a look at each unique code, a new algo trader can get an idea of the structure and complexity of each of the programming languages. This might help you make a decision on which language to pursue.

As an example, here is how simple Tradestation's Easy Language is. Suppose I want to buy the next bar if today's close is the highest close of the past 2 weeks (10 bars). In Easy Language, that becomes:

If close=highest(close,10) then buy next bar at market;

Not all languages are that simple!

Regardless of the method of programming, and the programming language you decide on, at some point you'll want to pick one method, and one platform, and get good at developing algos with it.

Of all the topics discussed in this section, I think this is the most important. Having a programming language you can easily learn, and feel comfortable with, is a big deal. Spend a lot of time upfront investigating what is best for you, and it will pay dividends down the road.

Integrating With Market Data

Most of the premier trading platforms these days integrate well with market data. Most require you to have a subscription with a 3rd party data provider, although others, such as Tradestation, have their own data.

Two important points to watch out for. First, make sure your data is delivered automatically and includes intraday data. Nothing is worse than having to schedule data downloads every evening. That used to be the norm back in the days of dial up modems, but in today's instant world, you should have immediate access to data.

Another important point is to make sure you trust both the data source and the platform. Not all data providers supply data to all platforms, so if you have a preferred data vendor in mind, your choice of platforms may be somewhat limited.

Market data integration is not a major point, but it is one that can trip you up if you ignore it.

Standard Indicators and Studies

Starting out with a new platform, the last thing you want to do is recreate standard technical studies like moving averages, RSI, ADX, stochastics, etc. You want to just reference them in your code, without programming them first.

Before selecting a platform, make sure it has a long list of indicators and functions already programmed in. Most platforms do, but it is always good to check first.

Programming Capabilities

Earlier I discussed the ease of programming, which I think is critical. But many times, programming might be easy because the language itself is limited in scope.

Some of the simple languages cannot do some of the complicated tasks you might require.

Tradestation, for example, is a good example of this. It uses a language called Easy Language, which is indeed easy. But since it was develop decades ago, primarily for backtesting, there are certain limitations with the language in today's computerized trading world. So, Tradestation now includes an additional language, Object Oriented Easy Language (OOEL), to provide a ton of additional capabilities. Of course, OOEL is a more complicated language as a result (FYI: I don't even use OOEL in my algo work).

MultiCharts platform has done the same thing as Tradestation, adding a new language in the .NET version of the platform.

If you have a complicated algo idea, and you are unsure if you can program it, I recommend you talk to experts at each vendor or in the software's user group, to see if what you need can be coded in the software.

Optimization

If your code has any parameters or numbers in it, for example the number of bars in a moving average, or the buy threshold in a RSI calculation, chances are at some point you will want to optimize that number. While too much optimization is definitely a bad thing, you at least will want the capability to do it in the software.

I consider this a must have, and most platforms provide this.

Walkforward Analysis

In my algo development work, I use a technique called walkforward testing to create "out-of-sample" results. These results tend to mimic live trading better than traditional "plug and chug" backtest optimizations.

Walkforward testing is an advanced topic, one that a new algo trader might not need right away. But it is a good feature for trading software to have. Otherwise, you may have to purchase a third party tool to conduct the analysis, or (gasp!) do the analysis manually. Having spent years doing it manually in the old days, I can safely say that manual walkforward testing is not a good long term solution!

Trader Community

Having a large and active trading community is critical for any software platform you choose. The technical support people at most software vendors are overworked, understaffed and most importantly usually not even traders. So, when you have questions, many times you will be talking to someone with less knowledge than you have!

If there is a strong community, there will be plenty of regular users willing and able to help you with questions. For example, I volunteer some of my time on the Tradestation user forum, and have contributed an average of 5 posts per week for the past 14 years to the community (over 3500 posts!). And there are a lot of others who help out even more than I do.

The other nice thing about a big user community is that there will also be a lot of code available for you to borrow. I have gotten some of my best ideas and algos from free code I have found on the internet. With a popular platform, chances are whatever you want to code has already been done for you, and you just might only need to modify it to suit your needs.

A vibrant community is a definite plus, and should be a very important part of your search criteria.

Live Trading & Automation

Once you create and test your algo, the last thing you want to do is convert it or move it to a different platform in order to trade it live or automate it. That, unfortunately, is still the case with some trading packages. These packages have not fully integrated the testing and actual trading pieces of their software.

You want a package that does it all: development, test and automated trading. If you settle for less than this, you will find yourself doing a lot of extra work eventually.

Picking a Platform – Conclusion

Hopefully in this chapter I have given you some things to think about as you pick a platform. There are obviously other important factors to consider (cost, availability in your country) that I have not mentioned, but I tried to highlight some of the big areas of concern.

There is no "one size fits all" solution, and while having many platforms to choose from is nice, it can be overwhelming. Don't let this dissuade you. Do some research, pick what you feel is the best choice, and then jump into it. The sooner you do that, the sooner you'll be creating trading algos!

CHAPTER 8 – POPULAR TRADING PLATFORMS

I n 2017-8, I asked readers of my blog to tell me which trading platform was their favorite. Here are the latest results:

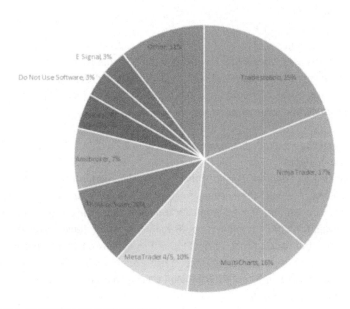

Figure 21 - Worldwide Survey, Trading Platforms

While the results of this survey are enlightening, I should point out that it is not a rigorous scientific survey. The results are probably a bit biased towards the top four – Tradestation, Ninja Trader, MultiCharts, and MetaTrader, since those are the primary platforms I use or have used. Many survey respondents are familiar with my work, so it follows that they might use the same software I do.

In any event, here is some more information on the top 7 choices selected by survey respondents:

Tradestation – www.tradestation.com

Overview, from https://en.wikipedia.org/wiki/TradeStation

"TradeStation Group, Inc. is the parent company of online securities & futures brokerage firms and trading technology companies. It is headquartered in Plantation, Florida, and has offices in New York, Chicago, Richardson, TX, London, Sydney and Costa Rica. TradeStation is best known for the analysis software and electronic trading platform it provides to the active trader and certain institutional trader markets that enable clients to design, test, optimize, monitor, and automate their own custom equities, options & futures trading strategies. TradeStation Group was a Nasdaq GS-listed company from 1997-2011, until acquired by Monex Group, a Tokyo Stock Exchange listed parent company of one of Japan's leading online securities brokerage firms."

Overview, from www.tradestation.com

"Tradestation Desktop

Buckle your seatbelt and prepare for an award-winning* trading experience.

Like a finely tuned race car, TradeStation's desktop platform delivers all the power, speed and flexibility active traders demand: dynamic market-scanning tools, fully customizable charting, fast and reliable trade execution, advanced order management and fully automated strategy trading.

It's all the professional-grade firepower you need to take on the markets with confidence.

TradeStation Analytics

Put the charting and analysis power of the TradeStation platform to work for you with TradeStation Analytics – without needing to open a brokerage account. This premium package offered by our affiliate, TradeStation Technologies, Inc., includes its award-winning desktop analysis platform and premium analysis tools such as the RadarScreen® real-time market monitoring and ranking tool, OptionStation Pro options analysis platform and the Portfolio Maestro portfolio-level strategy back-testing tool. You'll also receive real-time market data and access to TradeStation Technologies' massive historical market database, as well as mobile and web trading apps."

Full disclosure: I use Tradestation as my primary algo development and automated trading tool. It is not perfect, I sometimes have issues with it, but in the end, I am VERY satisfied with what it does and what it can deliver.

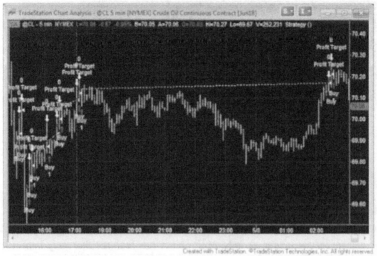

Figure 22 - Screenshot of a Tradestation Chart

NinjaTrader – www.ninjatrader.com

Overview, from www.ninjatrader.com

"STANDARD FEATURES

Advanced Charting, Trade Simulation, Strategy Backtesting, Real-Time Scanner, Market Playback, Custom C# NinjaScript Development

DATA, ADD-ONS & EDUCATION

Free EOD historical data for stocks, futures and forex, Choice of market data feeds including Kinetick, 1000s of 3rd party add ons, Free product training webinars, Media rich Help Guide, Hundreds of educational videos"

Full disclosure: I own a multi-broker lifetime license to NinjaTrader. I have done some strategy programming with it in the past, but currently I use it to help place automated trade orders at various brokerages. I have always been very pleased with their technical support.

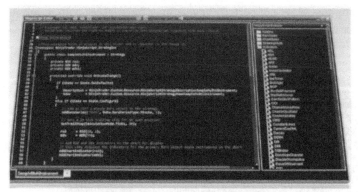

Figure 23- NinjaTrader Code Window

MultiCharts – www.multicharts.com

Overview, from www.multicharts.com

"MultiCharts is an award-winning trading platform. Whether you need day trading software or you invest for longer periods, MultiCharts has features that may help achieve your trading goals. High-definition charting, built-in indicators and strategies, one-click trading from chart and DOM, high-precision backtesting, brute-force and genetic optimization, automated execution and support for EasyLanguage scripts are all key tools at your disposal."

Full disclosure: I do not own MultiCharts, but I have used it and have tested it. It is similar to Tradestation, and most Tradestation Easy Language code easily converts to MultiCharts Power Language. If something bad ever happened to Tradestation, my backup plan would be to port all my algo strategies to MultiCharts.

MetaTrader4/5 – www.metatrader4.com

Overview, from www.metatrader4.com

"MetaTrader 4 is a platform for trading Forex, analyzing financial markets and using Expert Advisors. Mobile trading, Trading Signals and the Market are the integral parts of MetaTrader 4 that enhance your Forex trading experience.

MetaTrader 4 for Windows, Mac OS X and Linux powered PCs, as well as for iOS and Android mobile devices

Millions of traders with a wide range of needs choose MetaTrader 4 to trade in the market. The platform offers ample of opportunities to traders of all skill levels: advanced technical analysis, flexible trading system, algorithmic trading and Expert Advisors, as well as mobile trading applications.

Signals and Market additional services extend MetaTrader 4 frontiers. The Signals service allows you to copy trades of other traders, while the Market provides you with various Expert Advisors and Technical indicators that you can buy."

Full disclosure: I have MetaTrader 4, and use it to auto trade some forex instruments. I have only done a little programming with it, though.

Think Or Swim – www.thinkorswim.com

Full Disclosure: In house platform for the TD Ameritrade brokerage. I have never used it.

Amibroker – www.amibroker.com

Full Disclosure: I have never used this platform, but I have seen code from it, and it seems pretty straightforward. It also has some neat features many other platforms do not have. The prominent trading book author Howard Bandy uses Amibroker, along with Python (below).

Python, R and Matlab – www.python.org   www.r-project.org www.mathworks.com

Full Disclosure: I have used these programming packages a bit in non-trading activities. All are very flexible, and more and more traders/programmers are beginning to use them. I would consider them more programming platforms that can do trading, as opposed to pure trading platforms. If you want a bespoke, customized trading solution, one of these languages may be the best option.

CHAPTER 9 – TRADING PLATFORM – NEXT STEPS

O nce you have a trading platform selected, it is time to get to work! Before you can start creating and trading your algos, there are some specific platform tasks you need to master. Here is how I would do it, in the order I would recommend for you.

Learn The "Help" Sources Of Your Platform

Starting out with a new trading platform, whichever one it is, will certainly be a daunting task. You will need help. Luckily, if you choose one of the top platforms detailed in the previous chapter, you will find help in all sorts of places.

The first source of help should be the software vendor itself. They have trained people to answer most questions, especially for beginners. As you progress in your knowledge, though, you'll realize that other users are sometimes a better source of information. In the beginning, though, the vendor or their online help files and videos should be a first resort.

Once important thing to remember with vendor help – if it is a trade specific issue (missed order, bad fill, etc) you should always call the Trade Desk at your broker first. They are always the best source of information for specific trade details of your account. They might refer you to technical support, but when I have an issue and am unsure of my current position, I first call the Trade Desk.

Sometimes the vendor can't answer your question, or can't spend the time with you that you need. Luckily, there are 3rd party sources of technical assistance. For example, YouTube has a ton of useful videos for Tradestation. Many of these outside sources provide free information, along with paid services.

I think the true experts are the software users who are also traders. Make sure you know how to contact these people. Usually they can be found on trading forums like futures.io or elitetrader.com. Also, every software vendor has a user forum, where the best answers might come from experienced users and traders. I use Tradestation's user forum quite a bit, and I still ask questions to this day, some 14 years after I started using the software. The learning never ends!

Learn The Basics Of Your Platform

Don't make the mistake of trying to create an algo trading strategy the first day you start up your new trading software. Take some time, learn the basics, get a feel for how things are set up and how they work.

Be a child with the software. Have you ever watched a child interact with new software? I have with my three kids, and I can say, they are absolutely fearless. They will click on anything and everything, knowing they can usually shut the software down and start it up again fresh.

Be a kid – play with your new toy! Pull up a chart, throw some indicators on it, apply some canned strategies to the chart, and take a look at the resulting performance report. Explore and play – you will learn more quickly that way.

Learn The Basics Of Programming

Since most of your algo development will eventually consist of building strategies, learn how to do it! Start by learning the basic structure of the programming language – if...then statements, buy and sell order syntax, etc.

Each platform vendor likely has free manuals, reference guides, videos, etc. Most also have paid services, like introductory programming "boot camps." There are also plenty of third party companies with both free and paid programming tips.

But even with a comprehensive programming manual at your side, nothing can take the place of actually programming and practicing on your own.

Take a look at any strategies supplied with the software. Figure out what each line does, and how it is written. Make a copy of the strategy, and then modify the copy. Make small changes at first, and then progressively attempt more complicated changes.

Eventually, you will feel confident enough to build your own strategy from scratch. That might take a few days, weeks or even months, but that is where you eventually want to be – where you can easily modify existing strategies, and create your own new strategies.

Learn The Basics of Strategy Development and Evaluation

One major topic your software will not help you with is developing strategies in a proper manner. It is not as simple as applying a strategy to a chart, running a lot of optimization and then live trading the best overall optimized result. In fact, that is the exact WRONG thing to do, even though the software makes it so easy.

Correct strategy development and evaluation is a big topic, and there are very good books out there on proper strategy development. Books by Pardo, Tomasini and Davey are among the best for learning proper strategy development processes, in my opinion. I recommend you get a couple or all of these books, and incorporate their lessons into how you develop strategies.

Put it all together – Start with a chart, End with a strategy

Follow the steps in the next chapter, where I create a simple strategy. Although I use Tradestation for my example, you should be able to replicate each of the steps in your platform. Once you can easily do all these steps, you are in good position to begin creating your own trading algos.

Learn How To "Trick" Your Platform

The last task in learning your software is learning how to fool it. Almost every trading platform can be "gamed." That is, there are coding tricks and software settings that produce phenomenal equity curves. An example is below. I created this strategy in 1 minute. Looks perfect to trade, doesn't it? One slight problem, though – it is fake, and the results are based on exploiting the trading software backtest engine.

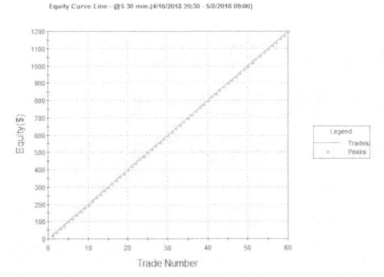

Figure 24 - Can You Create A Fake Algo Like This With Your Software?

Once you know a few ways to create fake, but perfect, looking equity curves, I'd say you know your software well enough. At that point, you know you are on your way to being an expert!

CHAPTER 10 – LET'S GET STARTED – A SIMPLE SAMPLE ALGO

I n this chapter, I am going to walk through a simple algo trading example. Note that my focus here is on using the trading software – regardless of the platform you use, you really must be able to do these basic tasks.

This example is NOT an example of the proper, or only, steps to develop a solid algorithm. That is beyond the scope of this short book. But this example will at least get you started with the concepts laid out in this book.

Treat this chapter as an interactive guide. For each step I take, try to duplicate it with your trading software. Go to the next step only when you have mastered the first step.

NOTE: This strategy, as presented, is NOT a tradable strategy – it has weak out-of-sample performance. It is merely an illustrative example. The steps shown do not represent the strategy development process I use for my own trading (my trademarked Strategy Factory® process). The key here is if you feel comfortable performing each of the steps I have detailed in this chapter, you have graduated from beginner algo level, and you can now be a serious algo strategy developer.

Call Up A Chart

Let's start out with a simple task. Open a daily continuous chart of Soybeans from 2007 to today. Have the start date of January 1, 2007 and end date of December 31, 2016.

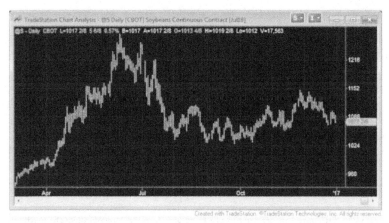

Figure 25- Can You Create A Chart Like This In Your Platform?

Get A Trading Idea

A simple trading idea is usually the best. In this case, I'll create a basic breakout system. The idea is that higher prices can only occur by exceeding previous high prices – pretty simple!

At the close of every bar, if the highest price is the highest closing price of the last "xbars," and the 15 bar ADX (a technical indicator measure of trendiness) is above 20, then go long. Do the opposite for short trades. I'll also include a simple stop loss, with no profit target (let winning trades run!). This type a system is good for trends, but will likely experience a lot of whipsaw during non-trending markets.

Program It

Program this simple strategy in your own platform. Code for Tradestation Easy Language is below. Include $5 round turn trade for commissions, and $25 round turn for slippage (VERY important!).

```
KJD2018-04 AlgoBook 02

input:xbar(10),sl(1000);

//ENTRY:  trade breakout of high/low close

  If high=highest(high,xbar) and ADX(15)>20  then buy next bar at market;

  If low=lowest(low,xbar) and ADX(15)>20   then SellShort next bar at market;

//EXIT:
  setstoploss(sl);
```

Figure 26 - Code This Strategy In Your Platform

Apply It To The Chart

Now, use your software to attach/apply that strategy to the previously built chart.

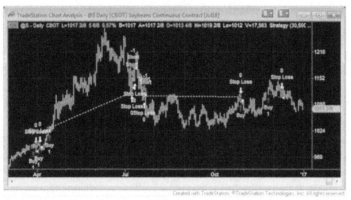

Figure 27 - Can You See Trades On Your Chart?

Optimize A Bit

Optimization is a dirty word, but when used in moderation it can be useful. Try to optimize the variable "xbar." Use a minimum value of 5 (short term) up to 30 (medium term) in steps of 5. Also, optimize the stop loss, from 500 to 1500 in steps of 500 dollars.

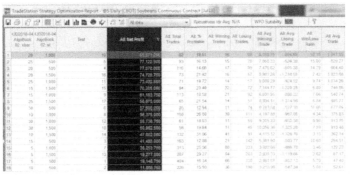

Figure 28- Optimization Results

Look At Results

Take a look at the optimization results. There are 18 iterations (runs), and all of them are profitable. This is generally a good sign. The dilemma becomes, which parameter set to choose? Highest Net Profit? Average Return on Account? Minimum Winning Percentage? Just ask that question in a trading forum, and be prepared for a slew of answers, with pointed and sharp opinions. The truth is there is no "perfect" criteria to use – it is a matter of personal preference and experience.

The choices for what to pick are pretty much endless, which is one reason I follow a set criteria when I do my development, which includes walkfoward testing.

For now, let's assume that we will pick a "median" Net Profit – not the best, not the worst. That is iteration #9, with value of xbar=30, stop=500.

Run Out-Of-Sample

Once we have our parameters chosen, it is time to run the strategy in 2017 and 2018. To do that, we simply change the chart end date, then review the updated Performance Report (not shown). The results, while not horrible (if 2017-8 results were really poor it would suggest we overoptimized or curve fit too much), are not really good enough for trading. At this point, the strategy should probably just be abandoned, since if we test again and again, our out-of-sample results are no longer truly out-of-sample.

Figure 29- Sample Strategy, Out-Of-Sample Results

Automate it

For this strategy, based on the out-of-sample performance, I would not trade it. But assume you wanted to trade it. What steps would you take to turn it on and automate it? Here is the step by step process for Tradestation:

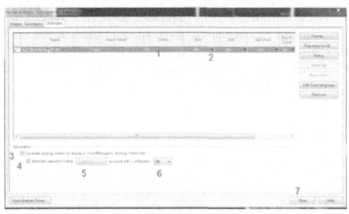

Figure 30- Steps To Automate A Strategy, Tradestation

CHAPTER 11 – TIPS FOR SUCCESSFUL ALGO TRADING

S uccessful algo trading, unfortunately, is a lot more than just learning a trading platform and a programming language. After trading algos in the futures markets for the last 25 years or so, here are some of my best tips on how to succeed. Hopefully they will help you, like they have helped me!

Have Realistic Expectations

Nothing is worse than the person with only $500 in his trading account who thinks he can make $50,000 per year via algo trading. Maybe one person in a million can do that, but the rest of us will never come close. Too many people enter trading with dollar signs in their eyes. Most end up blowing out their accounts.

Make sure, before you start trading, that you understand the potential rewards, but more importantly, the potential risks, inherent in algo trading.

Start With Enough Risk Capital

The amount of capital you start with can really influence your success rate. Traders with small amounts of capital run a higher risk of ruin, and that is a mathematical fact. In you only have a few thousand (or fewer) dollars in your trading account, here is what I recommend:

1. Trade with microforex (1/100 of a standard lot) at first. Don't worry about the money, worry about developing proper trading practices.
2. Gather more trading capital from outside sources. Get a second job, for example. Try to get your risk capital up to $10,000 or more, as a minimum. Give yourself a fighting chance against the professionals.

Learn Proper Strategy Development

Most people develop strategies incorrectly. They overoptimize, they curve fit, they have too many rules – the list of mistakes goes on and on. Learn how to develop strategies in a proper, time proven, scientific manner. Earlier, I suggested some authors who can help with that.

Test With A Lot Of Historical Data

Running a historical backtest on the last 3 months of market data is not enough. Markets continually change, and your algo strategy needs to be able to survive in most or all markets. So, you should test with as much data as you can. I generally test with about 10 years of data, and in some markets, more than 20 years.

Testing with many years of history makes finding a strategy much, much harder. But, it is the right thing to do. You want to find a long term edge, not a short term strategy that has worked for only the last 3 months – such "edges" might just be due to random luck.

Be Sure To Include Slippage and Commissions

I am amazed at how many people neglect commissions, and especially slippage, when they test a trading algo. The ironic thing is most strategies will show a profit, until you include these two frictional costs. Once these costs of trading are included, most strategies fail to make money.

The amount of slippage varies from market to market, but generally, for futures markets $25-50 per round trip trade per contract is a good rule of thumb.

Run Test With Out-Of-Sample Or Walkforward Periods

The education charlatans like to dazzle prospects with terrific looking equity curves. The key thing is most of those curves are based on optimized, in-sample data. They were optimized, so of course they look good!

For any algo you create, make sure you include an out-of-sample verification. Better yet, use the approach I employ, which is walkforward testing. Walkforward is a more complicated test method, but it gives you a lot of out-of-sample results to evaluate. This type of test is much more realistic than an optimized backtest.

Remember That Simple Is Usually Best

I remember a few years ago a Tradestation user was asking for advice for a new trading computer. He was lamenting the fact that his strategy took all weekend to optimize! He had about 300 variables he was optimizing, and he wanted to do it more quickly. I suggested instead of a new computer, maybe what he needed was a simpler strategy to test. He disregarded and mocked my advice, and soon disappeared from the trading community. Coincidence?

The fact is that simpler strategies tend to work better on unseen, future market data. Anyone can create enough rules to perfectly fit history, but these strategies almost never work in the future.

Keep your strategies simple. They won't look as good in backtest, but is that really the objective? Some misguided traders think it is, and they are wrong.

Know When To Quit

You will struggle with algo trading, we all have and will continue to. Trading is hard. So, you have to know when to change your approach, change your strategies, or just quit trading altogether. Have a plan for all the bad things that can happen. Then, follow that plan. Hopefully you'll never need it, but knowing when to quit is a requirement in this field.

I have heard too many sad stories of broken marriages, lost retirement accounts and financial struggles as a result of losing trading. Many of these may have been avoided if the person quit before things got too bad.

CHAPTER 12 –
CONCLUSION AND NEXT
STEPS

This short book has covered a lot of ground about the basics of algo trading for the retail trader. Trading is a tough world, but algo trading may just be a good route for your trading success. If you follow the steps detailed in this book, you might actually become as good as the professional traders you are competing against! It is hard work though, and never seems to get very easy. Remember that.

In conclusion, let's review the major steps you should take going forward.

Decide if Algo Trading is for You

Hopefully this book has given you a lot to think about, and you now know whether or not algo trading is for you. Don't try to force yourself to algo trade if it does not feel right. Good trading involves having the style of trading match the trader.

Pick Platform, Learn The Software

If you are serious about developing algos, pick a trading platform, learn to program with it, and start developing simple trading algos. The best way to learn this is by going out and actually doing it – hands on experience. Try to become a "professional" with your software package.

Learn Right Way to Build Strategies

A few times in this book I have mentioned how proper strategy development is a whole subject onto itself. Take some time, do some research, and search out experts in algo trading who are willing to share their methods. But be careful, most educators are charlatans. Ask for student references, look for independent verification of trading results, etc. Be skeptical – your algo career depends on doing things correctly.

You could also learn the way I learned:
1. Create an algo
2. Trade it live
3. Lose money when algo falls apart
4. Go back and modify the algo creation approach
5. Try again at step 1.

On second thought, maybe you shouldn't do it the way I did – it is way too expensive!

Build Some Strategies

You'll never know if you can algo trade unless you build some strategies. Learning the trading platform and programming is nice, but remember it is not the end goal. Many people fall into the trap of thinking it is. The end goal always has to be creating algorithmic strategies, and then trading them. Don't forget that!

Trade With Real Money

I know many wannabe traders who seem to have a lot of trading knowledge, but have very little actual real money trading experience. Just remember that eventually will you want to trade with real money. Many traders are afraid to. Don't fall into this trap.

At the same time, don't trade too early in your algo career, especially if you have limited funds. Many traders fall into this trap, and blow out their accounts before they really understand what is going on. Always remember that you want to be a professional trader, and always act with that in mind.

Review Performance, Make Changes

As you progress with algo trading, you will begin to get comfortable with a trading process, one which includes everything from strategy development to actual trading. A solid process is important, especially once it proves itself through market profits. Yet, at the same time realize that along the way you may need to update your approach, incorporate new advancements in algo trading, etc.

The best traders, whether they are discretionary or algo traders, retail or professional, all realize they need to continuously improve their trading, carefully monitor their performance and always strive to become a better trader.

*****

Successful algo trading is a long journey, and it can definitely be a profitable one, too. But just like any endeavor, it takes skill, patience and determination to succeed. Don't forget that.

With that, I'll say goodbye. I wish you the best in your algo trading. Feel free to drop me a line, and let me know how you are doing.

Thanks for reading, good luck and happy trading!

BONUS MATERIAL

Now that you've finished this introduction to algo trading, I have some nice book reader bonuses for you.

Simply go to www.AOKbooks.com and sign up for my Newsletter. I promise I won't spam you, and in return I'll give you the following great bonuses:

- All codes discussed in the book, along with workspaces, in Tradestation format
- A special starter trading strategy, fully disclosed – great for you to modify
- Invitations for free webinars and other events I put on
- Advance notice of new books that I write
- Some other algo trading goodies!

THANKS!

ABOUT THE AUTHOR – KEVIN DAVEY

As an award winning full time trader, and best-selling and award winning author, Kevin Davey has been an expert in the algorithmic trading world for several decades. Between 2005 and 2007, Kevin competed in the World Cup Championship of Futures Trading, where he finished first once and second twice, achieving returns in excess of 100% each year.

Kevin develops, analyzes, and tests trading strategies in every futures market from the e-mini S&P to crude oil to corn to cocoa. He currently trades full time with his personal account. He also helps small groups of traders significantly increase their trading prowess via his award winning algorithmic trading course, "Strategy Factory®." Kevin's Strategy Factory Workshop was awarded 2016 "Trading Course of The Year" by a prestigious trading website. More information is available at https://www.kjtradingsystems.com .

Kevin also helps educate the trading community via his best selling winning book, *"Building Winning Algorithmic Trading Systems: A Trader's Journey From Data Mining to Monte Carlo Simulation to Live Trading,"* published by Wiley. This book was a 2 time winner of TraderPlanet.com's "Trading Book of The Year" in 2014 and 2016.

Kevin is a Summa Cum Laude graduate of The University of Michigan, with a B.S.E in aerospace engineering. Kevin also has an MBA with Technology Management Concentration from Case Western Reserve University – Weatherhead School of Management, where he received the Dean's Academic Achievement Award with a perfect 4.0 grade point average.

Prior to trading full time, Kevin was Vice President of Quality and Engineering for an aerospace company that designed and manufactured flight critical components, managing over 100 engineers and support staff. For his efforts, he was honored with the prestigious "40 Under 40" Award from Crain's Cleveland Business Magazine.

Kevin currently lives outside of Cleveland, Ohio with his wife and three children.

Made in United States
North Haven, CT
08 April 2024

51065728R00046